HUMMINGBIRDS

Facts and Folklore from the Americas

Written by **Jeanette Larson** *and* **Adrienne Yorinks**
Illustrated by **Adrienne Yorinks**

iֱמi Charlesbridge

For Jim, who always reminds me to look for the beauty around us
—*J. L.*

For Wayne and Holly
—*A. Y.*

With much love and appreciation to these good friends and wonderful photographers who helped with this book: Alan Arkin, Suzanne Arkin, Douglas Schoenberg, William Vining, and Charles D. Winters.

Text copyright © 2011 by Jeanette Larson and Adrienne Yorinks
Illustrations copyright © 2011 by Adrienne Yorinks

Published by Charlesbridge
85 Main Street
Watertown, MA 02472
(617) 926-0329
www.charlesbridge.com

Library of Congress Cataloging-in-Publication Data
Larson, Jeanette.
  Hummingbirds : facts and folklore from the Americas / Jeanette
Larson and Adrienne Yorinks ; illustrations by Adrienne Yorinks.
    p. cm.
  Includes bibliographical references and index.
   ISBN 978-1-58089-332-9 (reinforced for library use)
   ISBN 978-1-58089-333-6 (softcover)
1. Hummingbirds. I. Yorinks, Adrienne. II. Title.
QL696.A558L37 2011
598.7'64—dc22   2010007578

Printed in Singapore
(hc) 10 9 8 7 6 5 4 3 2 1
(sc) 10 9 8 7 6 5 4 3 2 1

Illustrations done in fabric as fabric collage
Display type and text type set in Alcoholica and Goudy Oldstyle
Color separations by Chroma Graphics, Singapore
Printed and bound September 2010 by Imago in Singapore
Production supervision by Brian G. Walker
Designed by Diane M. Earley

"A lovely little creature moving on humming winglets through the air, suspended as if by magic in it, flitting from one flower to another, with motions as graceful as they are light and airy ..."

—John James Audubon, 1840

Table of Contents

FOREWORD

It was the summer solstice. I was enjoying the sunset from a balcony overlooking Mesa Verde National Park when a male broad-tailed hummingbird interrupted his mating display to check me out. He hovered less than a foot from my face. I could hear the metallic trill produced by the air passing through his tail feathers. After a minute or two, he resumed his hummingbird business: displaying for a potential mate, taking nectar from a nearby feeder, patrolling his territory, occasionally returning to his post in front of my face—near enough for me to feel just a little threatened.

I live in the Northeast where the ruby-throated hummingbird is the only breeding species. Eastern bird lovers all suffer from "hummingbird deficit disorder," an ailment that can be cured only by traveling to places where there are lots of hummingbird species. Birdwatchers willing to travel to the Western states might see twenty-one species, while determined souls who venture through Central and South America could bring that total to 332 species, if they're lucky. Hummingbirds are so addictive that Easterners like me take this cure as often as possible.

Part of my fascination is scientific—the arithmetic doesn't seem to add up. Like other neotropical migrants, hummingbirds spend only the breeding season in the United States, after which they fly to Central and South America. A ruby-throated hummingbird, which weighs about the same as a nickel, flies over five hundred miles nonstop to cross the Gulf of Mexico. With its high metabolism, how can such a tiny creature hold enough fuel to migrate this distance over open water?

The other part of my fascination is aesthetic. When seen in a certain light, a hummingbird's throat patch, or gorget, may appear to be brilliant iridescent red or blue or green. Seen from a slightly different angle, it looks dull black or colorless. The hummingbird's spectacular colors are produced by the way light refracts as it passes through the bird's feathers and are only partly caused by pigmentation.

Finally hummingbirds fascinate me because they can do things no other bird can. They are called hummingbirds because the speed of their wings, beating approximately eighty times per second, produces a low-frequency humming sound. High-speed wing beats and hyper-flexible shoulder joints enable hummingbirds to move their wings in figure-eight patterns, and this allows them to hover, fly backwards, and go from full speed to a full stop in a heartbeat.

I'm thrilled with *Hummingbirds: Facts and Folklore from the Americas*, which was created by my good friend Adrienne Yorinks and her book partner, Jeanette Larson. Adrienne's artistic sensibility and sense of color make her uniquely gifted in her ability to convey the quintessence of "birdiness." Like hummingbird plumages, Adrienne's quilts shimmer and seem to change color when viewed from different angles. They suggest movement and playfulness. Most of all I love her quilts because, like the hummingbirds depicted in them, they are beautiful. Adrienne and Jeanette's book conveys much interesting and valuable information about the science and the folklore of hummingbirds. *Hummingbirds: Facts and Folklore from the Americas* is a wonderful way to begin your own exploration of these magnificent creatures.

—*Wayne Mones*
Vice President, National Audubon Society

INTRODUCTION

Hummingbirds make up the second-largest group of birds in the Americas, so there are plenty of them around to observe. But look quickly! They're fast-flying birds.

The more scientists learn about hummingbirds—their ecology, behavior, flight patterns, and vocalizations—the better they understand them. Every aspect of their being seems to defy what humans think of as possible, and yet hummingbirds continue to surprise scientists and birdwatchers with their amazing feats. These passionate birds have a magical quality that inspires people to study and to write about them.

Because of people's fascination with these captivating creatures, in addition to scientific study, hummingbirds have also been the inspiration for legends and stories. Hummingbirds are found only in the Americas, so the legends and myths about them originate from Native cultures in North and South America. These stories, or pourquoi tales (*pourquoi* is French for "why"), explain why hummingbirds behave in a certain way or how these birds came to have specific physical characteristics. Pourquoi tales usually have some basis in fact but are expanded into stories and elaborated upon in retellings. Sometimes the stories are unique to one culture, but often they have passed among many different peoples. Although they may not be scientifically accurate, these tales describe a particular quality that adds to the intrigue of the birds.

To fully understand any subject, it's useful to gather knowledge about it through every discipline, whether factual resources or stories. For this book we've blended facts and stories, and we hope that the facts increase your hummingbird knowledge while the flavor of the tales enhances your appreciation of these lovely little creatures. In selecting birds for this book, we focused on those most common in North America and those that are distinctive or unusual. To write the tales, we read many versions of stories from various cultures and shortened them in our retellings. We hope this introduction to hummingbirds will lead you outside to find your own hummers and to continue to learn more about them.

—*Jeanette Larson and Adrienne Yorinks*

Hummingbird enthusiast, actor Alan Arkin

Size and Physical Characteristics

Hummingbirds are part of the order Apodiformes (ay-pod-uh-FORM-eez), meaning unfooted birds. There are three families in this order: hummingbirds, tree swifts, and swifts. The scientific name for the hummingbird family is Trochilidae (troh-KIL-uh-dee). The hummingbird family is divided into two subfamilies: Phaethornithinae (FEE-thorn-ih-thin-ee), or hermits, which has thirty-four species; and Trochilinae (troh-KIL-uh-nee), or typical hummingbirds, which has close to three hundred species.

Hummingbirds defy the limitations of their tiny size and other physical constraints that most species could not conquer. When early European explorers first saw a hummingbird, they thought it was a cross between an insect and a bird because of its small size. Hummingbirds weigh between 0.07 ounces (2 grams) and 0.70 ounces (20 grams). It would take almost fourteen bee hummingbirds, the smallest hummingbirds, to amount to just 1 ounce (28.35 grams). If you hold two pages of notebook paper, this is what the weight of an average hummingbird would feel like.

Like all birds, hummingbirds are warm blooded. Their metabolic rate, the speed at which they perform basic body processes, is the highest of any warm-blooded vertebrate in the animal kingdom.

A unique trait of hummingbirds, however, is that they are the only birds that can hover for prolonged periods in still air. Hummingbirds are most attracted to flowers that are large and tubular, but these flowers do not have a place for birds to perch. This is not a problem for the hummers, thanks to their ability to hover while feeding in mid-air. Hummingbirds feed for roughly two hours each day in order to maintain their amazing flight

abilities, and when they are not migrating, defending territory, or involved in courtship and breeding, they perch for the remaining active time, about sixteen hours. If they are inactive for a long period of time or if they are cold, hummingbirds enter a state called torpor, in which all their body processes slow down, in order to conserve energy.

Bill length and the shape of the bill vary between species of hummingbirds. Some have straight bills and some have sickle-shaped bills. They all lick nectar with their tongues in the same way but may visit slightly different types of flowers.

Compared to other birds, hummingbirds have rigid wings, short arms, long wing bones called hand bones, and short, weak legs. They have a remarkably flexible shoulder joint, which allows

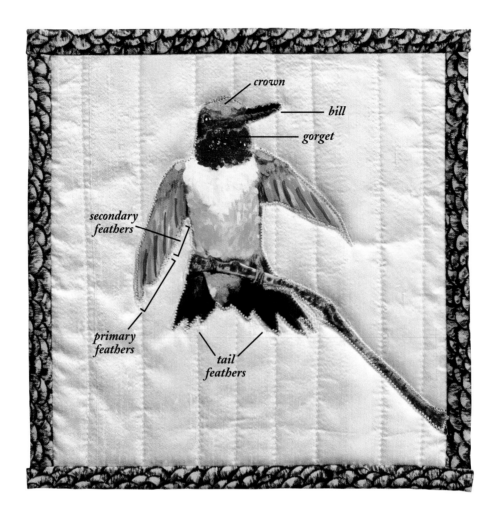

their wings to rotate almost 180 degrees. This accounts for their ability to hover while keeping their body motionless, much like a helicopter.

There is great variation in hummingbird plumage coloration. Males are more colorful than females in most species. Body feathers are basically black or rufous, a rusty brown color. The feathers of the colorful gorget (throat patch) and crown (top of the head) sparkle brilliantly when reflected by the sun. These areas are most pronounced in males and are used to signal rival males and to court females.

AN OHLONE LEGEND:
Why the Hummingbird's Throat Is Red

Several hummingbirds, including the ruby-throated hummingbird
(the most common species found in eastern North America)
and Anna's hummingbird (found in Central and Southern
California), have red or magenta feathers on their throats.
A legend told by the Ohlone, an indigenous people of the
central California coast, explains how this came to be.

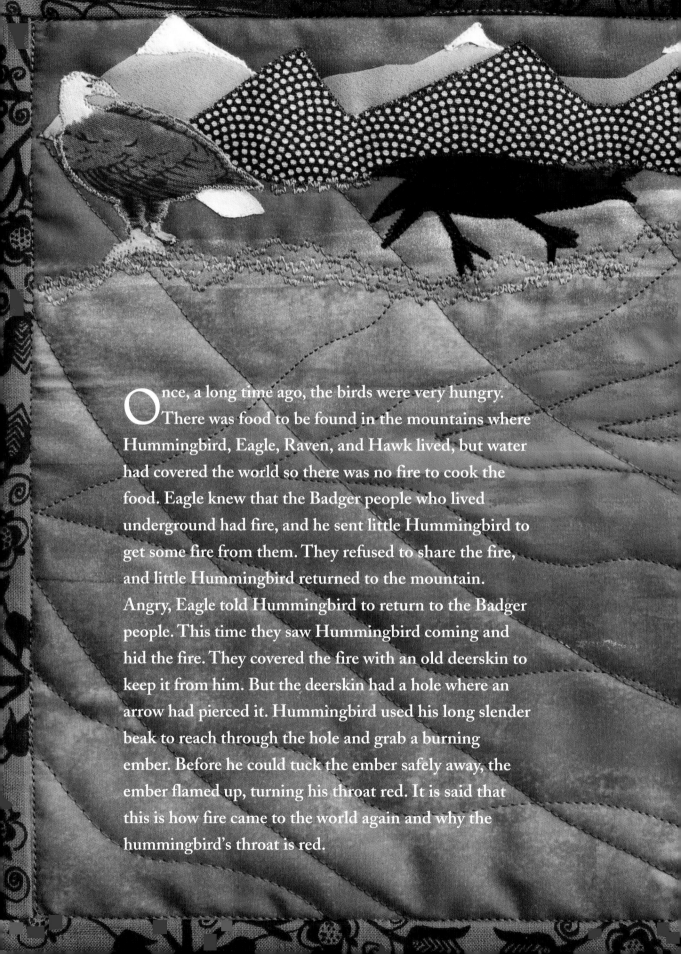

Once, a long time ago, the birds were very hungry. There was food to be found in the mountains where Hummingbird, Eagle, Raven, and Hawk lived, but water had covered the world so there was no fire to cook the food. Eagle knew that the Badger people who lived underground had fire, and he sent little Hummingbird to get some fire from them. They refused to share the fire, and little Hummingbird returned to the mountain. Angry, Eagle told Hummingbird to return to the Badger people. This time they saw Hummingbird coming and hid the fire. They covered the fire with an old deerskin to keep it from him. But the deerskin had a hole where an arrow had pierced it. Hummingbird used his long slender beak to reach through the hole and grab a burning ember. Before he could tuck the ember safely away, the ember flamed up, turning his throat red. It is said that this is how fire came to the world again and why the hummingbird's throat is red.

DIET AND FOOD

Hummingbirds must consume one-and-a-half times their body weight in nectar—an easily digested sucrose, or sugar, solution produced by flowers—each day to keep up their metabolic rate. Nectar is a mixture of water and sugar, so they consume half of their body weight in sugar daily. Imagine eating half of your body weight in candy bars every day! Although they get a lot of water from nectar, they occasionally drink water from leaves.

Hummingbirds fill their crop, a pouch in their throat for storing food, with nectar. They can eat, digest, and eliminate it from their bodies in less than fifteen minutes. This leaves them light and able to hover without having to carry undigested material in their bodies for a long period of time. Hovering requires lightness and is the most energy-intensive form of locomotion for any animal, which is why hummingbirds need to consume so many easily digestible calories. Compare the hummingbird diet with that of a vulture. Vultures will consume as much as possible when food is available. After gorging on carrion (the carcass of a dead animal) which requires

a long time to digest, vultures are so heavy that they cannot take off in flight for some time.

Hummingbirds also eat insects and spiders, which provide necessary protein, fats, vitamins, and minerals. Hummingbirds particularly need protein in order to grow new feathers every year.

Still, nectar is the most important part of the hummingbird diet. Hummingbirds have a brush-tipped, deeply split tongue, each side of which is rolled into a tube to lap up nectar at thirteen flicks per second. Hummingbirds are masters at finding nectar.

FINDING THE CHOICEST NECTAR

Hummingbirds have far better color vision than humans. They can see all the colors of the rainbow that we see, as well as ultraviolet colors. Colors in the ultraviolet spectrum are invisible to humans or else perceived as black. Some flowers develop ultraviolet patterns when they are most fertile, which is when they're richest with nectar. In addition to flowers with ultraviolet patterns, hummingbirds seem to prefer red flowers. Red flowers are easily seen in flight, particularly against a green background of foliage. Also, insects don't perceive red, so hummingbirds aren't in direct competition with insects for the nectar of red flowers. Scientists have found, though, that hummingbirds will adapt to any color flower that yields the best nectar in a given location. Hummingbirds have also evolved other behaviors to eliminate food competitors. They are active at first light, long before bees and other cold-blooded insects have warmed up enough to search for food.

Not only do hummingbirds have better vision than humans, but they also have an astounding memory. They remember which flowers they have already drained of nectar and pass over them. The following year during migration, however, they will visit the same flowers from the previous year. They also remember which bird feeders provided nectarlike sucrose. When you think about the rufous hummingbird, which migrates 2,500 miles (4,023 kilometers) each way every year, this is remarkable. The same hummingbirds might visit your feeder every year, so remember to keep it in the same location and make sure the sucrose solution is fresh and plentiful.

CATCHING PREY

Hummingbirds catch insects and spiders in two ways. They fly straight toward an insect with their bill agape so the insect goes directly to the back of their mouth, where they swallow it. They also hover around leaves and tree trunks and catch their prey by grasping it with the tip of their bill, tossing it into the air, and flying toward it to take it into their mouth.

TORPOR

If hummingbirds can't feed because of severe weather, they enter a state of torpor, or suspended animation, to conserve energy. In this state hummingbirds appear almost lifeless, similar to a bear in hibernation. Torpor is effective in conserving energy and body heat. Most hummingbirds have evolved the ability to control the level of their torpor because it makes them vulnerable to predators. As soon as they come out of torpor, hummingbirds stretch and then seek out food.

A Hitchiti Tale:
Why the Hummingbird Drinks Nectar

Although hummingbirds eat insects, most of the energy needed
to fuel their metabolism comes from the nectar they sip from
flowers. This story from the Hitchiti people in the southeastern
United States explains why hummingbirds drink nectar instead
of eating fish. You may see similarities between this tale and
"The Tortoise and the Hare."

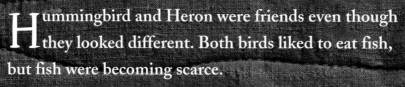

Hummingbird and Heron were friends even though they looked different. Both birds liked to eat fish, but fish were becoming scarce.

Hummingbird said, "There is not enough fish left for both of us. Let's race—whoever wins will own all the fish in the world."

Heron said, "Great idea! Let's race toward the big dead tree that lies on the bank of the river four days' distance from here."

"Agreed," said Hummingbird. "I will win because my wings beat swiftly."

Heron disagreed. "Mine are wider and will carry me farther."

On the first day of the race, Hummingbird was distracted by some flowers. When he saw Heron ahead of him, Hummingbird beat his wings to catch up. After flying for several hours, Hummingbird was exhausted and took a nap. He slept all night.

The next morning Heron was far ahead, as he had flown all night. Although Hummingbird flew like the wind, flapping his tiny wings so fast that the other birds couldn't even see them, the flowers and the promise of tasty nectar distracted him again.

For two more days, Heron flew slowly but steadily toward the big dead tree. When Hummingbird flew, he flew quickly, but he also stopped often to rest and to sip nectar. On the fourth morning, Hummingbird woke from his sleep and flew to the big dead tree, only to find Heron perched there waiting for him to arrive. From that day forward, Heron has eaten fish, and Hummingbird has sipped the nectar he so enjoyed during the race.

PLUMAGE AND COLOR

Hummingbirds have the highest density of feathers of any bird, exposing very little skin and thereby providing excellent insulation. To keep their plumage in good condition, they must preen themselves often. They preen by ruffling their feathers, scratching, combing, and bathing. They scratch and comb with their beak and claws, which helps to get rid of unwanted parasites. Hummingbirds keep their beaks clean by scraping them with their claws. Bathing seems to soften their feathers, making it easier to preen. Hummingbirds bathe by standing in shallow water, bobbing and splashing; perching near spraying waterfalls and sprinklers; diving into pools; rubbing up against wet leaves; and standing in the rain.

Each year hummingbirds molt, or lose their old coat of feathers. Molting makes it more strenuous for birds to fly and perform other activities, so hummingbirds have adapted so that they don't molt during migration. After they are situated in their new location, hummingbirds molt and generate a new coat. Molting also ceases when females begin to nest.

The famous naturalist John James Audubon described hummingbirds as "glittering fragments of the rainbow." Actually hummingbird feathers don't have much color. The refraction of light creates the brilliant, iridescent colors in their plumage. That is, the structure of the feathers splits light into its component colors, and certain frequencies are reflected back to the eye, making the viewer see brilliant colors.

A MAYA LEGEND:
How the Hummingbird Got Its Colors

Several legends explain how hummingbirds acquired so many colors. This one is from the Maya people of Mexico, who called the hummingbird Tzunuum (ZOO-noom).

When the Great Spirit first created Tzunuum, she was a tiny, delicate bird who possessed extraordinary flying skill. She was the only bird who could fly backward and the only one who could hover in the same spot. When the Great Spirit first created Tzunuum, she was very plain. Although her feathers had no bright colors, Tzunuum was humble and didn't mind that she was plain. Her only pride was in her flying abilities.

When it came time for Tzunuum to marry, she was disappointed to find that she had no wedding gown to wear. She was sad, and so her friends decided to make a beautiful dress and necklace for Tzunuum to wear on her wedding day. The vermillion-crowned flycatcher gave the red ring of feathers from around his throat. The bluebird offered several blue feathers for the gown, the cardinal gave red feathers, and turquoise and emerald feathers were provided by the motmot. A spider offered a veil of gossamer thread. All these pieces were sewn together.

When Tzunuum arrived for her wedding, she was surprised and happy. She was so humbled by the generosity of her friends that the Great Spirit sent word through his messenger, the sparrow, that Tzunuum should wear her wedding gown for the rest of her life. From that day forward, the hummingbird's feathers have been anything but plain.

FLIGHT

Hummingbirds are masters of aerial acrobatics, superior to any other bird. They can fly with their body held upright, unlike other birds, which fly parallel to the ground. Hummingbirds can also propel themselves backward, right and left, and even upside down. When hovering, their body is in a vertical position with fully extended wings. They don't "flap their wings" but rather fly by moving their rigid wings in figure-eight patterns parallel to the ground. Hummingbirds gain greater lift by spreading their tail feathers. Their upper-arm and forearm bones are very short, and their elbow and wrist joints can't move. Their shoulder joints, to which their wings are attached, can move in all directions, plus

Possible hummingbird wing positions during flight

24

rotate about 180 degrees. The rapid movement of their wings creates the birds' distinctive humming sound.

Hummingbirds start their flight before even leaving their perch. After only three wing strokes, they are almost at top speed, all in $^{7}/_{1,000}$ of a second! They propel themselves upward without the help of casting off from the perch. Imagine you are swimming laps in a pool, but as you end each lap, instead of using your legs, as most swimmers do, to push off from the side of the pool and gain momentum, you start each lap by using only your arms. It would be much more difficult and take much longer than $^{7}/_{1,000}$ of a second to get up to your top speed.

Large hummingbirds can reach up to twenty-five wing beats per second, whereas smaller hummingbirds have been observed at two hundred wing beats per second. Hummingbirds tend to maintain a steady speed while migrating and are fastest when defending their territory or performing a courtship dive to impress a potential mate. While performing his courtship ritual, an Allen's hummingbird dove sixty feet (eighteen meters) in approximately one second! Film footage revealed that he attained a speed of forty-five miles (seventy-two kilometers) per hour.

A West Indies Legend:
How the Hummingbird Won the Race

Over the years there have been many attempts to explain hummingbirds'
great flying abilities. This particular legend erroneously suggests that
hummingbirds hitch a ride on the wings of other birds to maintain high
speed and to fly great distances.

Many versions of this story exist, some featuring other birds as the
hitchhiker. This retelling is loosely based on a version from the West
Indies, but the presence of the puma suggests influence from stories
told in South America, where hummingbirds, condors, and pumas live.
While hummingbirds are one of the smallest types of birds, condors are
one of the largest. A condor's egg is larger than a full-grown hummingbird.

There was a time when two birds shared the blue skies. Hummingbird flitted about, hovering in the air with grace and ease. Condor's big broad wings lacked grace on the ground but allowed him to fly high and float on the wind. Small and large, the two friends played in the skies. Condor was so big that his wings blocked out the sun, casting a shadow over Hummingbird. Hummingbird would tease Condor about his size and boast that he could fly faster because he was smaller and quicker. Condor would laugh and say that they were both the same, except that he was big while Hummingbird was tiny.

One day Hummingbird found a windy tunnel. He boasted to Condor that he could get through the tunnel faster than Condor. Condor laughed, for he knew he was stronger and that his powerful wings would carry him forward while tiny, lightweight Hummingbird would be pushed back by the wind. Condor accepted Hummingbird's challenge, but when the time came for the race, Hummingbird was nowhere to be found. Condor laughed and boasted that he was already the winner. The other animals had gathered for the race, so Condor went to the starting line. Puma stood at the starting line and announced that the race would begin. Condor flew into the tunnel, flapping his wings. Just as he neared the end of the tunnel, Hummingbird came out from beneath Condor's feathers to easily win the race. Laughing, Hummingbird reminded his friend that it takes more than strength to get where you want to go. Condor reminded Hummingbird that he could not have won without help from a friend.

HABITAT

Truly all-American birds, hummingbirds are indigenous to the Western Hemisphere. Year-round, seasonally, or occasionally, they are found in North, Central, and South America—but nowhere else in the world. They live in every area of the Americas, ranging across Canada (from Yukon to Newfoundland and Labrador) in the north all the way to Argentina and Chile's shared region (called Tierra del Fuego) in the south. They can be found from the Juan Fernández islands in the Pacific all the way east to Barbados in the Atlantic. Their habitats include lowland forests, coastal mangrove swamps, deserts, subarctic meadows, and the snow line of the Andes.

Half of all hummingbird species live along the equator, where abundant flowers are available year-round. However hummingbirds also live in cold climates. Rufous hummingbirds nest in mountainous areas of the United States and Canada and migrate to Alaska to breed. English naturalist Charles Darwin watched a hummingbird called the green-backed firecrown flit around during snowstorms in Tierra del Fuego. British ornithologist G. T. Corley Smith found Chimborazo hillstar hummingbirds 15,000 feet (4,575 meters) up the Cotopaxi volcano in Ecuador. There, both hummingbirds and birdwatchers endure daily hail showers and nightly frosts. If caught unexpectedly in harsh weather, many hummingbirds enter a state of torpor to conserve energy and heat.

Why the Hummingbird Lives in the Mountains

Although hummingbirds live in many places, it's thought that they originated in the mountains around the equator before dispersing to other areas of North and South America. The Yamana people of Tierra del Fuego have an explanation for why hummingbirds live in the mountains.

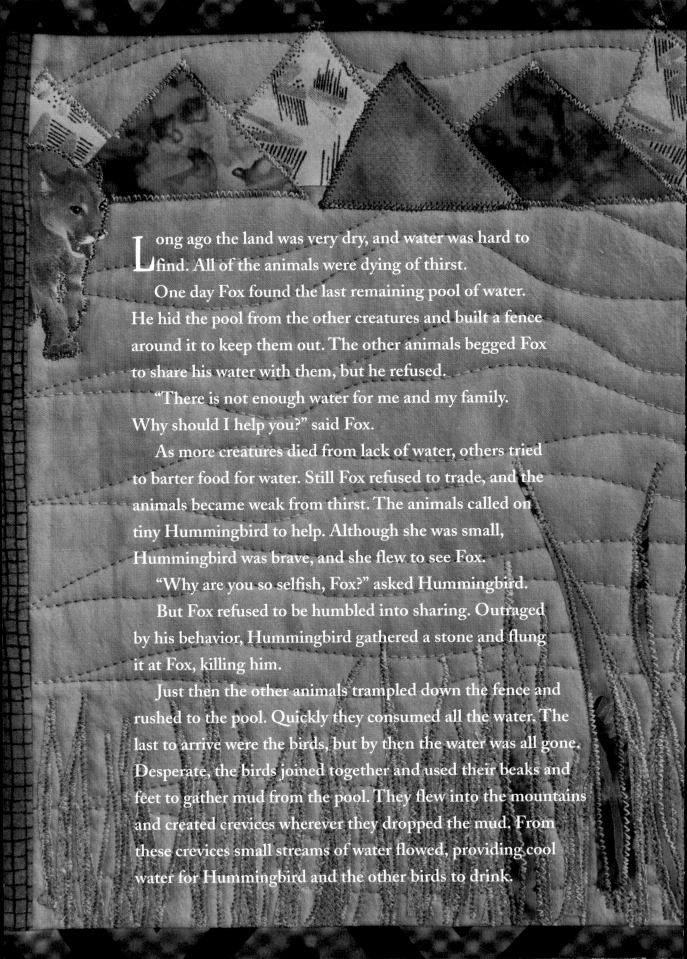

Long ago the land was very dry, and water was hard to find. All of the animals were dying of thirst.

One day Fox found the last remaining pool of water. He hid the pool from the other creatures and built a fence around it to keep them out. The other animals begged Fox to share his water with them, but he refused.

"There is not enough water for me and my family. Why should I help you?" said Fox.

As more creatures died from lack of water, others tried to barter food for water. Still Fox refused to trade, and the animals became weak from thirst. The animals called on tiny Hummingbird to help. Although she was small, Hummingbird was brave, and she flew to see Fox.

"Why are you so selfish, Fox?" asked Hummingbird.

But Fox refused to be humbled into sharing. Outraged by his behavior, Hummingbird gathered a stone and flung it at Fox, killing him.

Just then the other animals trampled down the fence and rushed to the pool. Quickly they consumed all the water. The last to arrive were the birds, but by then the water was all gone. Desperate, the birds joined together and used their beaks and feet to gather mud from the pool. They flew into the mountains and created crevices wherever they dropped the mud. From these crevices small streams of water flowed, providing cool water for Hummingbird and the other birds to drink.

MIGRATION

Changes in the length of the day are thought to trigger migration. Fall migration, when hummingbirds fly to warmer climates, is more leisurely than spring migration, when hummingbirds are rushing back to their nests. Fall migration for hummingbirds in North America takes place in late August or in September and is usually completed by October. Spring migration can start as early as February and continues throughout the spring to specific breeding grounds. Some tropical hummingbirds migrate between different habitats within the tropics so that they can visit different types of flowers to find better food sources.

Hummingbirds can fly long distances without stopping. Each species has its own migration strategy, and each bird migrates alone, rather than in a flock. Birds are generally safer when migrating in a flock, and it's remarkable to think that tiny hummingbirds fly all that way solo. In preparation for migration, which might include a twenty-hour nonstop flight, hummingbirds will gorge on insects and nectar to store fat, doubling their body weight in a week. Rufous hummingbirds have the longest migration of any hummingbird species, more than twenty-five hundred miles each way. They fly from central America to Alaska and back again. Ruby-throated hummingbirds migrate over two thousand miles each way from Panama to Canada flying five hundred miles across the Gulf of Mexico without stopping to refuel. Anna's hummingbirds are the only species that doesn't migrate.

An Aztec Legend:
Why the Hummingbird Migrates to Mexico

No one knows for sure where the Aztec people lived before they
came to what is now Mexico City, but this story offers one suggestion.
The chief god of the Aztecs was called *Huitzilopochtli* (wee-TSEEL-
oh-poach-tlee). He was also referred to as Hummingbird-on-the-Left
because he wore feathers from these tiny birds on his left foot.
According to legend, Huitzilopochtli could turn himself into a
hummingbird and show his people what route to take in their travels.
Another story of Huitzilopochtli is told later in this book.

Long ago the Aztec people lived in a land called Aztlan. One day a man heard a small bird singing in a tree. It was a hummingbird.

"Come. Let us go," said the hummingbird.

The man called another to join him and hear the bird speak. Again the hummingbird said, "Let us go."

The people took this as a sign that they should begin their journey out of Aztlan and move southward toward the land where the Maya lived. As they followed the hummingbird, the man asked, "How will we know where to stop?"

The hummingbird answered, "When we reach a beautiful place with rivers and mountains and forests, I will give you a sign. You will see an eagle perched on a cactus plant, eating a snake. That will be the sign that you have found your new homeland."

The Aztec people followed the hummingbird through lands that they thought were quite beautiful. But still they traveled farther. Eventually they reached a beautiful place in a green valley by a lake. There the Aztecs saw a golden eagle fly down from the sky and grab a snake from the marsh around the lake. As the eagle settled on a cactus plant to devour the snake, the hummingbird, who was really the god Huitzilopochtli, spoke. He told the people to build a great city at this spot. That city is today called Mexico City, and it might not exist had not the hummingbird led the people there.

COURTSHIP AND REPRODUCTION

The breeding period for most North American hummingbirds occurs during spring and summer after migration. Males arrive first, and they quickly establish individual territories. Females arrive soon after the males and immediately begin nesting. After a female has completed her nest, she will choose her mate. Males perform courtship displays to attract females.

Courtship behavior consists of song or sound, plumage exhibition, and dazzling aerial flights. Each species of hummingbird has developed a specific pattern of behavior to attract a mate and to keep the species alive. As a general rule, male hummingbirds have the most beautiful coat, while female plumage is drab. This is well suited to the roles they play in courtship, reproduction, and nesting. Male hummingbirds need a brilliant coat and showy flying to attract a potential mate, while females, being the primary defenders of the chicks, are plain in order to help camouflage themselves and to protect their young from predators.

When male hummingbirds enter a courtship dive, they orient their iridescent feathers toward the sun in order for their feathers to look their most vibrant. Scientists have found that male hummingbirds rarely do this on cloudy days, implying that hummingbirds seem to be conscious of the effect of light on their feathers.

Aerial stunts often include swoops, dives, and acrobatics, accompanied by specific vocalizations. An Anna's hummingbird may begin a dive toward his mate from 150 feet (46 meters) in the air, stop midair to sing while peering down at her, and then dive straight toward her at top speed while emitting loud metallic popping sounds. Scientists believe that the males' tail feathers, not their vocal organ, create the popping sounds. Other species have adapted courtship rituals called shuttle flights, which usually take place in heavy undergrowth. Here the male performs a series of short flights in front of his mate, swinging back and forth while emitting either a form of vocalization or a vibration of his feathers. After these wondrous displays, a chase usually occurs between the male and female, ending in mating.

NESTS

Nest building takes a few days to two weeks and varies greatly between hummingbird species. Nests also reflect the individual

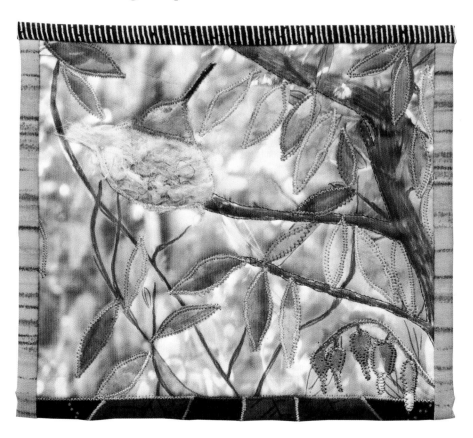

female's creativity and what materials she has on hand. Scientists have found all kinds of animal hair, plant fiber, as well as fibers from the roofs of abandoned cars, in hummingbird nests.

Whether female hummingbirds build their nest in a tree, hanging from a ledge, or clinging to a rock, they make it by using their beak and feet to weave plant fibers into a cone or cuplike shape. They use sticky spider webs and their own saliva to glue the nest together, and fill the cup with fluff from plants such as silky milkweed. Cobwebs are also used to connect the nest to the base of a branch or a foundation. Female hummingbirds flatten the floor of the nest by running and jogging on it. The nest is built to protect the eggs and growing hatchlings from the elements. Some hummingbirds breed during the rainy season, so an insulated nest is particularly important for them. Much the same way that we insulate wires with plastic to protect them in a storm, organic materials such as hair and plant down insulate the nest from electrical storms. Female hummingbirds cover the outside of their nest with bits of lichen, bark, and moss. The nest is pliable and will bulge and flatten to accommodate the growing hatchlings.

EGGS AND CHICKS

Female hummingbirds generally lay two eggs each, a day or two apart. Hummingbird eggs are quite small, measuring less than a half inch (1.27 centimeters) in diameter, the size of a small jelly bean. Female hummingbirds incubate their eggs for fifteen to twenty-two days, keeping them warm by gently sitting on them with fluffed-out feathers. The females periodically turn the eggs with their beak for even incubation.

When a chick is ready to hatch, it first pokes its head through the shell and then begins to emerge into its new world. It's now called a hatchling or nestling. Hatchlings are born blind and without feathers, so their mother works hard to shade her babies with her wing on hot days and keep them warm when the weather is cold or rainy. Within eight to twelve days, the hatchlings are able to maintain their own body temperature. Nestlings need to be fed up to three times each hour and begin to beg for food almost immediately. Female hummingbirds feed their young the same diet they eat, insects and nectar. The mothers feed them by regurgitating their catch directly into the babies' gaping mouths. They also must protect their young from numerous predators at all times and keep the nest clean. Female hummingbirds are kept very busy.

Hummingbird chicks appear alert at around sixteen days and start to preen their feathers and stretch their wings in preparation for flight. When they stretch their wings, they are called fledglings. Other species of fledglings may need to be nudged from the nest, but not hummingbirds. When hummingbird fledglings are ready to leave, they usually choose morning hours to take their first flights. Most are proficient fliers almost immediately, although some have difficulty maintaining height or learning to land properly. After several trial flights, the fledglings are ready to leave the nest.

A Taino Story:
Why the Hummingbird Is Attracted to the Color Red

Plant nectar is clear and colorless, but hummingbirds are attracted more frequently to red and yellow flowers. The Taino people of Puerto Rico tell a love story to explain why hummingbirds are attracted to red flowers more than other flowers. Like Romeo and Juliet, two young people in love are forbidden by their families to marry. In order to be together, one becomes a hummingbird and the other a red flower. Today the *colibri*, or hummingbird, is considered sacred by the Taino people.

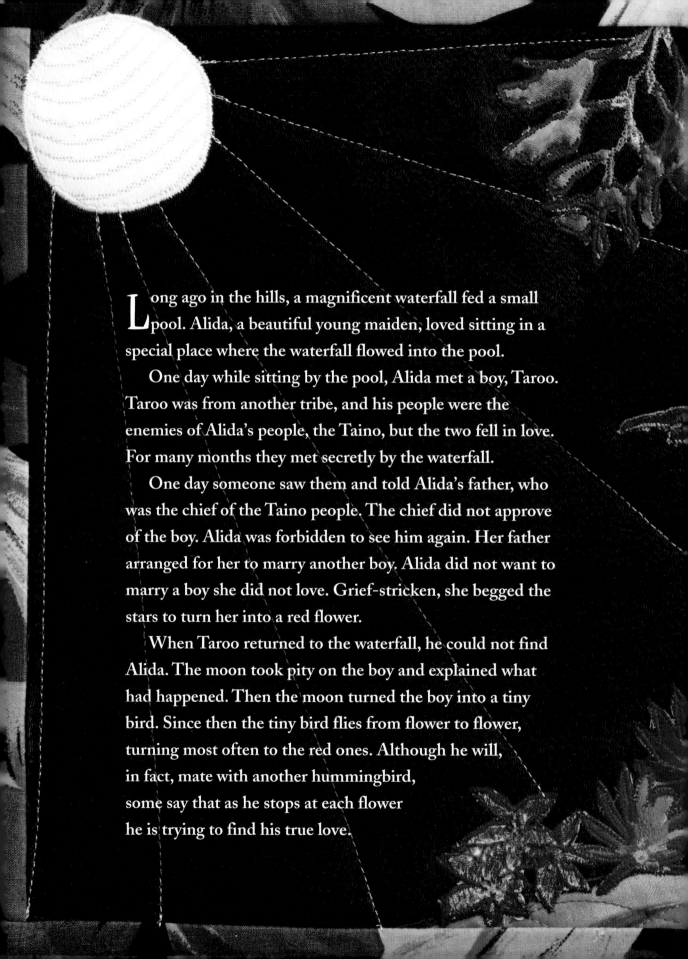

Long ago in the hills, a magnificent waterfall fed a small pool. Alida, a beautiful young maiden, loved sitting in a special place where the waterfall flowed into the pool.

One day while sitting by the pool, Alida met a boy, Taroo. Taroo was from another tribe, and his people were the enemies of Alida's people, the Taino, but the two fell in love. For many months they met secretly by the waterfall.

One day someone saw them and told Alida's father, who was the chief of the Taino people. The chief did not approve of the boy. Alida was forbidden to see him again. Her father arranged for her to marry another boy. Alida did not want to marry a boy she did not love. Grief-stricken, she begged the stars to turn her into a red flower.

When Taroo returned to the waterfall, he could not find Alida. The moon took pity on the boy and explained what had happened. Then the moon turned the boy into a tiny bird. Since then the tiny bird flies from flower to flower, turning most often to the red ones. Although he will, in fact, mate with another hummingbird, some say that as he stops at each flower he is trying to find his true love.

VOCALIZATION

Most kinds of birds are born with the sounds that they use.
Only four of the twenty-three major groups of birds must learn
to make sounds: songbirds, parrots, lyre birds, and hummingbirds.
Occasionally one species of hummingbird will even learn to imitate
another species' sounds or songs.

Hummingbirds are noisy and are often heard before they are
seen. They chatter, produce guttural sounds, whistle, and chirp,
sometimes at higher frequencies than humans can hear. Of the
more than three hundred hummingbird species in existence,
only three have beautiful songs—the wedge-tailed sabrewing,
the vervain hummingbird, and the wine-throated hummingbird.
The other species make unappealing sounds; one species' song
was even compared to the sound of a nail being scratched on
a rusty can! Songs are used mostly by male hummingbirds to
attract females and to protect their territory.

A Navajo Story:
Why the Hummingbird Has No Song

Although hummingbirds do have a voice, the Navajo people tell
this story to explain why hummingbirds don't have a beautiful song
like most other birds.

The People say that when the world was new, all the birds were alike. All sang the same songs and wore the same plain feathers of gray or white or brown.

In the early days hummingbirds were the same size as the other birds, and they ate seeds and berries. Hummingbird awoke early each day and ate as soon as he was awake. He kept eating and eating, for he was always hungry. The other birds scolded him for eating more than his share and for taking food that was needed by other birds. To avoid being scolded, Hummingbird started to awaken earlier and earlier, and he ate more and more.

Angered, the other birds decided that Hummingbird was too big. If he were smaller, Hummingbird would need less food.

And so, the People say, Hummingbird began to shrink. His beak thinned and grew longer as his body shrank. His thin beak allowed him to pull nectar from flowers. As he enjoyed the nectar, leaving the seeds and berries for the other birds, he tried to sing out in happiness. But his body had shrunk and he had become so small that only a squeak emerged from his mouth; he had no song. The People say that this was punishment for being such a greedy eater, but the birds took pity on Hummingbird. If he could not have a beautiful song, Hummingbird would have beautiful feathers.

PREDATORS

Hummingbirds are inquisitive, quarrelsome, and territorial. Part of each day is spent in defense, and they are constantly vigilant. Their small size makes hummingbirds vulnerable to many predators, but they aggressively defend themselves, their food sources, and their territory. Given the opportunity, small hawks, roadrunners, snakes, and lizards will kill and eat hummingbirds. Leopard frogs and freshwater bass have been known to drag them underwater. Even spiders, praying mantises, and dragonflies are a threat. Aerial displays and vocalizations can act as a deterrent to unwanted intruders, including other hummingbirds, but if this doesn't work, hummingbirds are fearless warriors and will attack predators much larger than themselves. Hummingbirds' best defense, however, is their speed and agility. With their quick maneuverability, alert hummingbirds can even escape the clutches of a viper.

An Aztec Legend:
Why the Hummingbird Is a Fearless Warrior

Some hummingbirds are fierce protectors of their territory, chasing
other birds away from bushes and plants that they consider their own.
Although a certain amount of their aggressive behavior is a bluff,
their small size makes them appear to be very brave when they
defend themselves and their nest.

Long ago the Aztec people lived in a beautiful place called Aztlan. Many other people envied the place and also wanted to live there. They attacked the Aztec people, trying to drive them away from the land.

Huitzilopochtli, the Aztec leader, fought valiantly to defend their territory, and he turned back many attackers. But just as the last battle was ending, an arrow hit Huitzilopochtli, killing him.

The Aztec warriors saw their leader fall but could not stop to help him, as the enemy found new strength and the Aztecs had to continue defending their land. When the battle ended, the warriors looked back to find their leader, but he had vanished. In his place they saw only a hummingbird whirring around the very spot where Huitzilopochtli had fallen. They knew that this was the spirit of their hero, for his beak was long like a sword, and he darted fearlessly through the sky, protecting himself and his territory. Huitzilopochtli became a god to the Aztec people, and he would one day lead them to a new land in Mexico.

From that day forward the Aztec people believed that their fallen warriors were transformed into hummingbirds. These birds roam the fields, sharpening their fighting skills and staying ever alert for predators and danger.

Conclusion

Hummingbirds have been objects of fascination for centuries. Though fossil evidence is scarce because of the fragility of their bones, the existence of hummingbirds is documented in pre-Columbian artifacts and artwork. A giant, three-hundred-foot-long, hummingbird drawing that stretches across the Peruvian plateau dates back to the Nazca civilization, which prospered from 200 BCE to 600 CE. Other ancient rock drawings and stone carvings depicting hummingbirds survive from civilizations that are now extinct. We know very little about these ancient people, but we can gather that they were as fascinated by hummingbirds as we are.

Most remarkable, of course, are the hummingbirds themselves. They have survived for millennia, adapting over time to their changing environment, and bringing great beauty to our world. In our time the pace of change on the planet has greatly accelerated because of the influence of human beings. Radical climate changes, human encroachment, and habitat destruction are putting a huge burden on all life on earth, making the survival of more delicate species of birds such as hummingbirds much harder. Though tenacious, hummingbirds are still small birds, dependent on the environment for their survival. We need to be vigilant so that hundreds of years from now, when other children are studying hummingbirds, they will still be able to see these remarkable creatures with their own eyes.

GLOSSARY

Apodiformes In the biological classification system, the order of birds to which hummingbirds belong

Aztec A collective name given to the seven tribes of Nahuatl-speaking people that ruled Central Mexico at the time of the Spanish conquest in the 1500s; name given to any member of the Aztec nation

breed To produce offspring

chatter To make rapid short sounds that are inarticulate and indistinct

courtship The act of performing certain social activities with the intention of attracting a mate

crop A pouch on birds' throats that serves as a receptacle for food

crown The top of the head

fledgling A young bird that has the feathers needed for flight

flock An assembly of birds that group together

gorget A colorful patch on the throat

hatchling A young bird that has just emerged from its egg

Hitchiti Native American peoples who settled along the Ocmulgee River in Georgia around 1000 BCE. They were considered part of the Creek Confederacy—a group of different native peoples who inhabited Georgia and Alabama. In the 1800s many of these peoples joined either the Seminoles in Florida or Creek Nation, which was later removed to Oklahoma due to the Indian Removal Act.

hover To hang suspended in the air, generally remaining in place

hummingbird Any member of a family (Trochilidae) of nectar-sipping birds found only in the Americas

indigenous Having originated and lived in a specific area; native

iridescent Having a brilliant, lustrous, or colorful appearance

lift An upward force that opposes the pull of gravity, allowing birds to climb higher in the air

locomotion The act of moving from one place to another

Maya Mesoamerican peoples living in Mexico and Central America whose origins date back to 1500 BCE. Their ancient civilization developed the only true system of writing in the Americas.

metabolic rate The amount of energy used within a given period of time

migrate To move from one area or climate to another on a regular schedule, usually for the purpose of feeding or breeding

molt To shed feathers that will later be replaced by new growth

Navajo (Diné) Native American peoples who primarily live in Arizona, New Mexico, and parts of Utah. They call themselves "Diné," meaning "the People," and they settled in the Southwest around 1400 CE.

Nazca An extinct pre-Incan civilization from Peru that dates back to 200 BCE; a city in Peru; a desert in Peru. The Nazca Lines are geoglyphs, or ground drawings; many people believe that the Nazca people created these lines.

nectar An easily digested sucrose, or sugar, solution produced by flowers

nestling A young bird that is not yet ready to leave the nest

Ohlone Indigenous peoples of Northern California. They call themselves Muwekma, meaning "the People." Dating from the sixth century, the Ohlone were originally made up of fifty distinct tribes instead of a united nation. Today the Ohlone include members of the Muwekma Ohlone, Rumsen, and Mutsun tribes.

perch To stand or rest on an elevated place

Phaethornithinae In the biological classification system, one of the two subfamilies to which hummingbirds (family Trochilidae) belong; includes hermit and other hummingbirds that are not considered to be "typical hummingbirds"

plumage The collective term for the feathers covering a bird

pourquoi tale From the French word meaning "why," these folktales explain why something is the way it is, especially natural phenomena

predator An animal that lives by hunting and seizing other animals for food

preen (for a bird) To clean and straighten feathers with a beak or bill

refraction The turning or bending of a ray of light as it passes from one medium (such as air) into another of different optical density

regurgitate To bring back up; to vomit

rufous A reddish-brown color

sickle Having a curved shape

song Vocal sounds and signals produced by birds, distinguishing them from other bird species

songbird A bird that has a particularly melodious song or call

sucrose A sugar found in many plants

Taino An extinct Arawakan group originally from Puerto Rico and areas of the Caribbean. Taino chiefdoms thrived from 1200 CE until the time of the Spanish conquest.

territory An area or tract of land that one or a group of animals use for feeding, mating, and nesting, and which they will also defend against intruders

torpor A state in which an animal's body slows down to conserve energy, similar to hibernation

Trochilidae In the biological classification system, the family to which hummingbirds belong

Trochilinae In the biological classification system, one of the two subfamilies to which hummingbirds (family Trochilidae) belong; sometimes called "typical hummingbirds"

ultraviolet Light waves beyond violet in the spectrum and not visible to humans

vocalization The production of sound; an utterance or song

whistle To produce a shrill, sharp musical sound

Additional Reading for Kids

Arnold, Caroline. *Birds: Nature's Magnificent Flying Machines.* Watertown, MA: Charlesbridge, 2003.

Baker, Keith. *Little Green.* New York: Harcourt, 2001.

Collard, Sneed B., III. *Wings.* Watertown, MA: Charlesbridge, 2008.

George, Kristine O'Connell. *Hummingbird Nest: A Journal of Poems.* New York: Harcourt, 2009.

Kelly, Irene. *It's a Hummingbird's Life.* New York: Holiday House, 2003.

Kirkland, Jane. *Take a Backyard Bird Walk.* Lionville, PA: Stillwater, 2001.

Ryder, Joanna. *Dancers in the Garden.* San Francisco: Sierra Club, 1994.

Thompson, Bill, III. *The Young Birder's Guide to Birds of Eastern North America.* New York: Houghton Mifflin/Harcourt, 2008.

Bibliography

Holmgren, Virginia C. *The Way of the Hummingbird.* Santa Barbara, CA: Capra Press, 1986.

Long, Kim. *Hummingbirds: A Wildlife Handbook.* Boulder, CO: Johnson, 1997.

Klesius, Michael. "Flight of Fancy," *National Geographic*, January 2007, pp. 114–129.

Williamson, Sherri. *A Field Guide to Hummingbirds of North America.* Boston: Houghton Mifflin, 2002.

Tale Sources

Although a variety of sources, including many websites, were consulted in creating a version of each legend, these books were invaluable resources.

Caduto, Michael J. *Earth Tales From Around the World.* Golden, CO: Fulcrum Publishing, 1997.

Curry, Jane Louise. *The Wonderful Sky Boat: And Other Native American Tales of the Southeast.* New York: McElderry, 2001.

Holbrook, Florence. *Why the Crocodile Has a Wide Mouth and Other Nature Myths.* New York: Dover, 2004.

Holmgren, Virginia C. *The Way of the Hummingbird.* Santa Barbara, CA: Capra Press, 1986.

Long, Kim. *Hummingbirds: A Wildlife Handbook.* Boulder, CO: Johnson, 1997.

Malotki, Ekkehart. *The Magic Hummingbird: A Hopi Folktale.* Santa Fe, NM: Kiva, 1995.

Palacios, Argentina. *The Hummingbird King: A Guatemalan Legend.* Mahwah, NJ: Troll, 1993.

Ramirez, Michael Rose. *The Legend of the Hummingbird: A Tale from Puerto Rico.* New York: Mondo Publishing, 1998.

Searcy, Margaret. *Race of Flitty Hummingbird and Flappy Crane: An Indian Legend.* New Orleans: Portals, 1996.

Yamane, Linda. *When the World Ended, How Hummingbird Got Fire, How People Were Made: Rumsien Ohlone Stories.* Berkeley, CA: Oyate, 1995.

RESOURCES

(all websites accessed February 7, 2010)

Birding Organizations

American Birding Association
http://www.americanbirding.org/
Catering to recreational birders, this group offers specific services and resources for young birders.

American Bird Conservancy
http://www.abcbirds.org/
This organization encourages the preservation of native wild birds and their habitats.

The Hummingbird Society
http://www.hummingbirdsociety.org/
Based in Sedona, Arizona, this organization supports activities to protect hummingbirds, particularly those species that are threatened with extinction.

Hummingbirds.net
http://www.hummingbirds.net/
This site, maintained by an avid hummingbird bander (a person trained to place a tiny numbered band on the leg of a hummingbird so that scientists can study its habits and migratory patterns), includes information on hummingbird species, festivals, facts, and research, including migration maps.

National Audubon Society
http://www.audubon.org/
With chapters in each state, the group strives to conserve and restore natural ecosystems for birds and other wildlife.

Southeastern Arizona Bird Observatory (SABO)
http://www.sabo.org/
A nonprofit organization dedicated to the conservation of the birds of southeastern Arizona, this group allows you to adopt your own hummingbird.

Wild Birds Unlimited
http://www.wbu.com/
This chain of retail and online stores helps establish feeding habitats. Their projects encourage education about birds, and they support scholarships for children to attend wildlife camps.

HUMMINGBIRD SANCTUARIES

Although you can often see hummingbirds in your own backyard, there are many places where hummingbirds gather, making them easier to observe. Listed here are a sample of sanctuaries and aviaries, but there are also many smaller gardens where hummers gather, and local festivals that spotlight hummingbirds during migratory periods.

Arizona-Sonora Desert Museum, Tucson, AZ
http://www.desertmuseum.org/

The Baiting Hollow Hummingbird Sanctuary, Long Island, NY
http://www.lihummer.org/

Chihuahuan Desert Research Institute, Ft. Davis, TX
https://cdri.org/index.html

Kern River Preserve, Weldon, CA
http://audubon.org/local/sanctuary/kernriver/

Lincoln Park Bird Sanctuary, Chicago, IL
http://www.chicagoparkdistrict.com/index.cfm/fuseaction/custom.natureOasis14

River Lake Inn, Colon, MI
http://www.riverlakeinnrestaurant.com/

Strawberry Plains Audubon Center, Holly Springs, MS
http://www.msaudubon.org

WEBSITES

Birdwatching for Kids
http://www.biglearning.com/treasurebirds.htm
Everything you need to get started, including tips for helping children get
involved in bird-watching.

Enchanted Learning
**http://www.enchantedlearning.com/subjects/birds/printouts/
Hummerprintout.shtml**
Print out a coloring sheet for the ruby-throated hummingbird.

The Great Backyard Bird Count
http://www.birdsource.org/gbbc/kids
Play games or do serious science research by helping to count birds each
February.

Hummingbird Habitat
http://www.birdwatching-bliss.com/hummingbird-habitat.html
Learn how to create a school or backyard habitat to attract
hummingbirds.

Just for Kids
http://www.audubon.org/educate/kids/
Check out the hummingbird camera, find your state bird, and listen to
bird songs.

ART NOTES FOR *HUMMINGBIRDS:*
FACTS AND FOLKLORE FROM THE AMERICAS

The fabric collage illustrations in this book were created with cotton, silk, fabric paint, acrylic paint, photo transfers, glitter, and thread. They were stitched together in much the same way that nonfiction information and hummingbird folklore were woven together to create this book— we wanted our readers to gain both scientific knowledge and cultural nuances about hummingbirds in order for them to more thoroughly enjoy these spectacular flyers.

It's difficult even for seasoned birdwatchers to classify some species of hummingbirds. One reason is because hummingbirds are so fast that it's hard to catch a glimpse of any identifying markers. Another reason is that they can breed with other species of hummingbirds, creating one-of-a-kind hybrids. Finally, juvenile males and females can appear much different from what they will look like as adults. So we've tried to show the essence of the characteristics of each species depicted in this book (also see the page-by-page hummingbird identification guide below).

We hope our book inspires readers to go outside and view hummingbirds in their own backyards.

Front cover: swallow-tailed hummingbird; Back cover: blue-throated hummingbird; Title page: Calliope hummingbird; p. 7: Allen's hummingbird; p. 9: violet sabrewing; p. 10: ruby-throated hummingbird; p. 11: ruby-throated hummingbird; p. 13: Anna's hummingbird; p. 14 (top left): broad-billed hummingbird; p. 17: white-eared hummingbird; p. 19 (bottom right): buff-bellied hummingbird; p. 21: broad-tailed hummingbird; p. 23 (top left, to the right of the spider): hybrid female hummingbird; p. 25: Calliope hummingbird; p. 27: black-chinned hummingbird; p. 29 (bottom left): great sapphirewing; p. 31: magnificent hummingbird (female); p. 33: rufous hummingbird; p. 36: rufous hummingbird; p. 39: black-chinned hummingbird; p. 41: chicks, Costa's hummingbird (female); p. 43: Calliope hummingbird; pp. 44–45: green-breasted mango; p. 47: two green violet-ear hummingbirds; p. 48 (top left): Anna's hummingbird; p. 50: golden-breasted puffleg; p. 51: two ruby-throated hummingbirds; p. 53: sword-billed hummingbird

INDEX